Starters for
A Level Language

by

Sarah Aynsley

NATE

Starters for A Level Language is published by the National Association for the Teaching of English (NATE), the UK subject teacher association for all aspects of the teaching of English from pre-school to university.

NATE
50 Broadfield Road
Sheffield
S8 OXJ
Tel: 0114 255 5419
Fax: 0114 255 5296
email: info@nate.org.uk
web: www.nate.org.uk

ISBN: 978 0901291 98 1

Printed by GB Print & Design
Quorn House
Charnwood Business Park
North Road
Loughborough
Leicestershire
LE11 1LE

Contents

Acknowledgements

We are grateful to the following for permission to reproduce extracts:

Bloomsbury Publishing for extract from *The Man with the Dancing Eyes* by Sophie Dahl
The Women's Press for extract from *The Color Purple* by Alice Walker
Methuen Publishing Limited for extract from *A Taste of Honey* by Shelagh Delaney
The Guardian newspaper for extract from review *Under her Spell* by Nicholas Lezard © Nicholas Lezard, The Guardian, 28 June 2003

Introduction

This collection of starter activities is aimed specifically at students making the transition from GCSE English language to AS Level English Language or English Language and Literature.

So the activities are starters in two ways. Firstly, they are lesson starters: short, sharp 10-15 minute tasks to introduce and reinforce linguistic concepts. Secondly, they are for students who are 'starting' AS Level language.

The objective of the pack is to make aspects of linguistic study at AS and A Level more accessible. It does not attempt to oversimplify the concepts but allows students to touch the 'first base' of language analysis.

With an acknowledgement to the Key Stage 3 strategy for some design features, the activities can be starters, fillers or part of a plenary. They are flexible and can be developed as much or as little as required. Additionally, the resources for each starter are intended to be practical and economical. Many can be simply written on the white board or copied on to an overhead transparency. It is taken for granted that teachers will use a variety of strategies to enhance delivery of the exercises e.g. using paired discussion or small groups, creating games and competitions, presenting them through ICT or using mini whiteboards (they are highly recommended for checking comprehension), requiring purely spoken or sometimes written answers.

All the lesson starters are based on the assessment objectives for AS Level English Language. They cover the main areas in four sections: grammar/syntax, lexis/semantics, phonology and graphology.

Unit One   Grammar & Syntax

Lesson 1   Lexis and Function

Definitions/Key words   **lexical** or **content** words: related to the real world, both physical and abstract

function or **grammatical** words: meaning related to function in a sentence

Activity 1   Put the following words onto cards and take one each. You must describe your word, without spelling it or referring to the number of letters, and try to get the other students to guess it: **novel, fiction, a, genre, the, prose, at, pen, poet, for, leaflet, in**

Were some words more difficult than others? Why? What do you notice about the words that you struggled with?

Activity 2   Look at these extracts from the West Midlands Safari & Leisure Park Guide Book. Which words are missing? How meaningful are they? Can you fill in the gaps? What happens in the second paragraph?

Located _____ _____ heart _____ rural Worcestershire, West

Midlands Safari _____ Leisure Park covers _____ area _____

almost 200 acres _____ _____ ideal place _____ spend

_____ day _____ _____ family... Take _____ safari- _____ 'll

believe _____ 're _____ Africa _____ no time, particularly _____

_____ drive-around _____ African Lion, White Rhinoceros _____

Elephant Reserves.

The_____ _____ _____ _____ over _____ _____, _____,

and _____ _____ to _____ _____ from _____, _____ and

_____, _____, _____ and _____.

Activity 3   Try to complete the following table.

	Example from Text	Lexical Word	Function Word
Nouns	*Worcestershire*	✓	
Verbs			
Adverbs			
Prepositions	*in*		✓
Adjectives			
Determiners			
Conjunction			

Lesson 2   Word Classes

Definitions/Key words   **word classes**: all words can be classified into categories related to their function within a sentence. The main ones are: **nouns, verbs, adjectives, adverbs, determiners, pronouns** or **deictics, prepositions** and **conjunctions**.

Activity 1   Remind yourself of the word classes by going through the extract from *The Man with the Dancing Eyes* by Sophie Dahl. Write down examples of each of the main word classes shown above.

> In the golden half-light of a midsummer's evening, the sort where any kind of magic can occur, and often does, in the midst of a party held in a wild and rambling garden, stood Pierre, teetering on highly unsuitable heels, surrounded by a symphony of overripe roses.
>
> Nobody was quite sure where she came from or exactly what it was she did.

Activity 2   Look at the statements below. Try to match them up with the word classes above.

- …modify nouns and pronouns
- …change tense
- …can be modal or auxiliary
- …decide the meaning and use of a noun
- …consist of the definite article and the indefinite article
- …indicate relationship
- …can be a substitute for a noun but can't be premodified
- …can change the intensity of a sentence
- …connect clauses
- …can be personal or possessive
- …can have a determiner and premodification or postmodification

Activity 3   In pairs, take a word class and try to evaluate how vital it is. What happens to a sentence if you take away the verbs, conjunctions…?

Lesson 3   Verbs & adverbs, active & passive

Definitions/Key words

active voice: where the focus of the sentence is the subject performing the action of the verb (e.g. *the girl kicked the ball*)
passive voice: where the focus of the sentence is the recipient of the action described by the verb (e.g. *the ball was kicked by the girl* or, more anonymously, *the ball was kicked*)

Activity 1

Which of these sentences are in the passive voice and which are in the active voice? How does it affect your perception of the text and meaning in each sentence?

The glass was held by Sheila's small elegant hands.	Sheila's small elegant hands held the glass.
The black tuxedo jacket was buttoned by Dwain.	Dwain buttoned the black tuxedo jacket.
The champagne was poured.	Sheila poured the champagne.
The door of the red sports car was slammed.	Dwain slammed the door of the red sports car.

Activity 2

Sheila poured the champagne purposefully.
Adding an adverb to the sentence can change the meaning. As in this case, the action of pouring the champagne becomes more significant and the reader begins to contemplate why the action might be occurring. Add a different adverb to each of the sentences in activity one and explain what effect this has in each case.

Activity 3

Read the extract below. Comment on the description used in this passage. Note down a list of the verbs which connect to a) Sheila and b) Dwain. What do you notice about Sheila's part in this interaction?

> Sheila stood elegantly on the balcony with a crystal champagne glass in her hand. She could sense his dominant approach as he left the bustling party to join her.
> "I thought I might find you out here." The husky American drawl and scent of aromatic cologne revealed his identity immediately. She spun round as he grabbed her arm with his strong masculine hands.
> She blushed furiously. "Dwain...what are you doing here?" He said nothing but pulled her closer. She could now clearly see his chiseled features and remembered why she had fallen for him so many times before. Sheila trembled, "Take your hands off me..." but before she could finish, he kissed her passionately.

Lesson 4   Modal verbs

Definitions/Key words

modal verbs: auxilary verbs which express the possibility and likelihood of events, e.g. may, must, shall

Activity 1

Put the following verbs into categories of your choice and then explain why you chose to order them in that way.

jump	hate	will	dance
hurt	need	stand	eat
must	walk	look	love
run	might	can	shall

Activity 2

You may have noticed that in terms of their function they fit into two main categories: full verbs and auxiliary verbs. The auxiliary verbs are all linked to the possibility or likelihood of an event happening. These are called modal verbs and include:

will, shall, may, might, would, can, could, must, ought to

Look at the following sentences and place each of the modal verbs in the space. What happens to the meaning of each sentence in each case?

Discipline is a problem. Children ...... behave.
There's an old lady struggling with a heavy bag. I ...... help.

Activity 3

Look at the following example of a political speech in which the speaker aims to encourage the electorate to vote for her. How has she used modal verbs to try and influence her audience?

I am addressing you today with our hopes for tomorrow. We ought to have safer streets. We should be able to walk around our neighbourhood after 9 o' clock without being frightened for our lives. We must have law and order...and we will!

Lesson 5   # Morphology

Definitions/Key words

morphology: the study of the form and structure of words in the English language

morpheme: the smallest unit of lexical or grammatical meaning which cannot be further subdivided

Activity 1

Create word families by attaching affixes to any of the following words: **path, act, graph, part.**

> e.g. **path**: empathy, empathetic, antipathetic, pathology, pathological, pathos, pathetic, pathogen, sympathy, sympathetic

Activity 2

Which of these words contain free morphemes which can stand alone without the affix?

misogynist	microfiche	monogamy	organism
misdemeanour	microscope	monotheism	valediction
misanthropy	venomous	specious	immediate
unionism	judicious	intangible	dispensation

Create your own word list, to test a discussion partner.

Activity 3

Now, focus specifically on affixes (e.g. **able, ible, ing, ive, pre, ify, ally, ly, sion, tion, less, ful, ism,** etc.) which change word classes and list as many combinations as you can find.

e.g. **verb + able = adjective**   *(enjoy + able = enjoyable)*

Lesson 6   Breaking up text

Definitions/Key words   sentence, clause, phrase

Activity 1   Listed below are the elements used to build text. However, they are mixed up. Match the words correctly to their definitions.

- **morpheme:** a group of words without a finite verb
- **clause:** the smallest unit of lexical or grammatical meaning which cannot be further subdivided
- **phrase:** an isolable unit of meaning
- **word:** a sequence of words which can stand alone and make sense
- **sentence:** a group of words which includes a subject and a verb

Activity 2   Have a go at building up text to a paragraph, starting from the word given below.

Morphemes	un+forgive+able
Word	unforgivable
Phrase	
Sentence	
Paragraph	

Activity 3   Examine the extract from opening of Mansfield Park. Comment on the sentences, clause and phrases used by Austen. What do you notice about their length, content, and punctuation?

About thirty years ago, Miss Maria Ward of Huntingdon, with only seven thousand pounds, had the good luck to captivate Sir Thomas Bertram, of Mansfield Park, in the county of Northampton, and to be thereby raised to the rank of a baronet's lady, with all the comforts and consequences of an handsome house and large income.

Lesson 7   Sentences

Definitions/Key words

simple sentence: has only one clause (e.g. *The garden was absolutely beautiful.*)

compound sentence: has two or more clauses which are coordinated (e.g. *The garden was a mess and he felt daunted by his task.*)

complex sentence: has at least one subordinate clause as well as the main clause (e.g. *As soon as he arrived, he began to clear up, dumping all the rubbish on the heap.*)

Activity 1   Look at the two extracts overleaf. What type of sentences are used? Are they complex, simple or compound? What do you notice about the length of the sentences and the punctuation?

Activity 2   You will have noticed that in the two extracts the sentences are mainly declarative. Why is this the case?

Sentences have different functions: they can be declaratives (statements), interrogatives (questions), imperatives (commands), or exclamations. Fill in the table below with three examples of each one and what effect they might have.

Functions	Example	Effect
Declarative		
Interrogative		
Imperative		
Exclamatory		

Activity 3   The audience and purpose of text may determine the types of sentences that are used. Think about each of the following examples. What types of sentences might be used in each one? Explain the reasons for your thoughts.

1) Instructions on the back of a shampoo bottle.
2) A script for a TV soap.
3) A warning label on a bottle of bleach.
4) A pre-1914 novel.
5) A charity leaflet appealing for donations.
6) A theatre programme.

Extract 1

Within a short walk of Longbourn lived a family with whom the Bennets were particularly intimate. Sir William Lucas had been formerly in trade in Meryton, where he had made a tolerable fortune and risen to the honour of knighthood by an address to the King, during his mayoralty. The distinction had perhaps been felt too strongly. It had given him a disgust to business and to his residence in a small market town; and quitting them both, he had removed with his family to a house about a mile from Meryton, denominated from that period Lucas Lodge, where he could think with pleasure of his own importance, and unshackled by business, occupy himself solely in being civil to the world. For though elated by his rank, it did not render him supercilious; on the contrary, he was all attention to everybody. By nature inoffensive, friendly and obliging, his presentation at St. James's had made him very courteous.

Pride and Prejudice, Jane Austen

Extract 2

Often described as a psychotropic or mind-altering drug, a psychoactive drug is a chemical substance that changes one's thinking, feelings, perceptions and behaviour. These changes are the result of the drug's action on the human brain. Among the psychoactive drugs are those classified as follows:

Narcotics- powerful painkillers, the narcotic analgesics also produce pleasure feelings and induce sleep.

Depressants- drugs also known as sedatives that slow down the central nervous system function, relax or tranquillize the person, and produce sleep.

Drugs In Modern Society

Lesson 8   Syntax

Definitions/Key words   **syntax:** the grammatical arrangement of words in language

Activity 1   Examine the following three sentences.
What is unusual about the syntax in each case?

I would I were a pine tree deeply rooted,
And thou the lofty, cloud-beleaguered rock.
(*Love in Exile*, Mathile Blind)

Unhappy that I am, I cannot heave
My heart into my mouth.
(*King Lear*, Shakespeare)

Down the close, darkening lanes they sang their way
To the siding shed,
And lined the train with faces grimly gay.
(*The Send-Off*, Wilfred Owen)

Activity 2   Explore how the structure of the sentence can be manipulated to foreground (bring into prominence) a particular feature or element. Look at the following imaginary newspaper headlines. Explain what you think has happened to the word order in each case and what effect you think this has.

Drunken MP dead!

Alcohol kills drunken MP!

Drunken MP killed by alcohol!

Activity 3   Summarise what happens to the meaning when the sentence structure is altered. Write the first paragraph to a newspaper article with one of the above headlines, continuing from that viewpoint.

Alternatively, analyse an entire newspaper article to examine how syntax can affect how the reader interprets the meaning.

Lesson 9   Cohesion

Definitions/Key words

cohesion: the grammatical, lexical and phonological techniques used to 'stick' a text together.

anaphoric reference: a word or phrase which refers to a previous part of the text.

cataphoric reference: a word or phrase which refers ahead to another part of the text.

Activity I

Listed below are nine different techniques for making a text cohesive. Decide whether they are examples of grammatical cohesion, lexical cohesion or phonological cohesion. Do any of the techniques fit into more than one category?

- Substitution of pronouns for nouns.
- Use of conjunctions to link ideas.
- Consistent rhyme scheme.
- Use of assonance or alliteration.
- Repetition of a word or idea.
- Use of tense.
- Syntactical parallelism.
- Subject-specific lexis.
- Anaphoric and cataphoric reference.

Activity 2

Susie lifted the lid off the dustbin. She didn't find what she had expected. Amongst the pile of rotting vegetables, empty tin cans and crumpled cellophane lay a shape. First, it stretched a limb, pulling back sharply as it collided with the black plastic enclosure. Then, beneath some shreds of carrot skin and a cardboard milk carton, she saw an eye – it blinked, opening and closing long black eyelashes, almost winking at her.

Text mark and label this text with examples from the above list.

Activity 3

Write the next paragraph of that text and annotate it with examples of cohesive devices.

Lesson 1	# Denotation & connotation

Definitions/Key words

semantics: concerned with the study of meanings
denotation: linking directly or precisely
connotation: linking obliquely or indirectly

Activity 1

The word red denotes a colour. However, it has many connotations which include passion, anger, caution and love. Look at the following denotations of car makes and note down the associations that you make.

Make of Car	Denotation	Connotation
Renault Clio	Small, mid-range	usually driven by females, often second family car
Robin Reliant	economical, three-wheeled	
Vauxhall Vectra	family saloon	
Red Ferrari	expensive sports car	
Bentley	luxury range, powerful	

Activity 2

Connotation means the association that society or the individual places on a word. Therefore, a word or phrase may mean many different things depending on who attaches meaning to it.

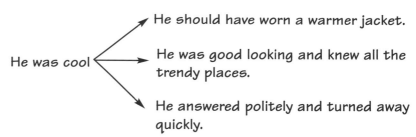

He was cool
- He should have worn a warmer jacket.
- He was good looking and knew all the trendy places.
- He answered politely and turned away quickly.

Now think of three alternative connotations of:
She was on fire.

Activity 3

Examine the description of Shug Avery taken from *The Color Purple* by Alice Walker. What do you think the author suggests about this character through the connotations of her appearance?

> She got on a red wool dress and chestful of black beads. A shiny black hat with what look like chickinhawk feathers curve down side on cheek, and she carrying a little snakeskin bag, match her shoes.

13

Lesson 2   Lexical sets

Definitions/Key words

Lexical sets: groups of words that are associated by meaning

Activity 1

> When starting Ju Jitsu it is essential to have your own gi as you need this for many of the throws and grabs. When you are competing, you must rei into the dojo and also to the sensei, who may be a shodan or nidan. You can tell who he or she is by the hakama they wear over their gi.

This extract of text contains subject specific vocabulary. The reader needs to have some knowledge of the subject in order to make sense of it. Make a list of the words which belong to the lexical set of Ju Jitsu, a Japanese martial art.

Activity 2

Lexical sets can be broken down further into categories **hypernyms** and **hyponyms**. For example, a hypernym such as furniture can be categorised into the hyponyms wardrobe, desk, table and chair.

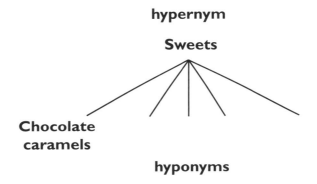

hypernym

Sweets

Chocolate caramels

hyponyms

Add some of your own hyponyms to the hypernym *sweets*. Now do the same for the *weather*.

Activity 3

Examine the poem *To Autumn* by John Keats on the next page. One of the lexical sets is associated with nature. Find these hyponyms in the poem. Which other lexical sets can you identify in the poem?

J. Keats

CCLV. Ode to Autumn

SEASON of mists and mellow fruitfulness,
Close bosom-friend of the maturing sun;
Conspiring with him how to load and bless
With fruit the vines that round the thatch-eaves run;
To bend with apples the moss'd cottage-trees,
And fill all fruit with ripeness to the core;
To swell the gourd, and plump the hazel shells
With a sweet kernel; to set budding more,
And still more, later flowers for the bees,
Until they think warm days will never cease;
For Summer has o'er brimm'd their clammy cells.

Who hath not seen thee oft amid thy store?
Sometimes whoever seeks abroad may find
Thee sitting careless on a granary floor,
Thy hair soft-lifted by the winnowing wind;
Or on a half-reap'd furrow sound asleep,
Drowsed with the fume of poppies, while thy hook
Spares the next swath and all its twinèd flowers:
And sometimes like a gleaner thou dost keep
Steady thy laden head across a brook;
Or by a cyder-press, with patient look,
Thou watchest the last oozings, hours by hours.

Where are the songs of Spring? Ay, where are they?
Think not of them, thou hast thy music too,—
While barrèd clouds bloom the soft-dying day
And touch the stubble-plains with rosy hue;
Then in a wailful choir the small gnats mourn
Among the river-sallows, borne aloft
Or sinking as the light wind lives or dies;
And full-grown lambs loud bleat from hilly bourn;
Hedge-crickets sing; and now with treble soft
The redbreast whistles from a garden-croft;
And gathering swallows twitter in the skies.

Lesson 3   Etymology

Definitions/Key words   **etymology:** the study of the origin and development of words

Activity 1   Scan the text taken from a cosmetics bottle. Make a list of the words that are recognisable from the English language even if they are spelt differently.

> **Récipient sous pression. A protéger contre les rayons solaires et à une temperature superieure a 50°. Ne pas vaporiser vers une flamme ou un corps incandescent. Conserver à l'écart de toute flamme ou source d'eétincelles ou d'ignition - No pas fumer. Conserver hors de la portée des enfants. Eviter de vaporiser vers les yeux, ou sur une peau irritée et d'inhaler intentionnellement. Ne pas utiliserpour un usage autre que celui pour lequel le produit est destine. Ne pa utiliser dans une atmosphere confinée.**

Activity 2   Use a good dictionary to locate the exact origin of each word, e.g. *Latin, Greek…* and write these next to each one. What ideas do you have about the origins of the English language that we use today?

Activity 3   Language is constantly changing and developing. To explore this idea, look closely at an extract from a Shakespeare text and find as many words as you can which:

• have changed their spelling over time,
• have changed their meaning over time.

Lesson 4   Blends and compounds

Definitions/Key words

compounds: entire words are combined to form a new expression, such as **goose + bump = goosebump**

blends: parts of a word are combined together to give a new word, such as **fan + magazine = fanzine**

Activity 1

Cut up the cards and match the words which compound together to make other words. Think of others to write on the blank cards, or invent your own.

card	town	
base	loud	
step	black	
cross	data	
egg	house	
board	word	
bird	daughter	
mouth	shell	

Activity 2

Cut up the cards and match the words which blend together to make other words. Invent your own blends and write them on a blank card for a partner to work out which words you have combined.

motor	snow	
helicopter	breakfast	
execute	recorder	
skateboard	hotel	
guess	monologue	
lunch	travel	
estimate	camera	
airport	electric	

Activity 3

In *Jabberwocky* by Lewis Carroll, there are many examples of blends. Carroll blends **flimsy + miserable** to create the word **mimsy** and **gallop + triumph** to create the word **galumph**. One reason he does this is to reinforce the fantastical nature of his poem. List other reasons why blends and compounds are created.

Lesson 5   Word play

Definitions/Key words

homographs: words which have one spelling but two pronunciations and two distinct meanings or usages, e.g. wound
conversion: when a word fits into more than one word class, thus having more than one meaning, e.g. *a subject* (noun) and *to subject* (verb)

Activity 1

Explain to your teacher or talk partner what is unusual about the lexis in each of the following statements.

1. The bandage was wound around the wound.
   e.g. The word 'wound' is a homograph: in this sentence it is both a noun, the wound, and the past tense of the verb, to wind.

2. She was content with the content of the package.

3. She made a record of her collection of records.

4. He refused to take out the refuse.

Activity 2

Word play is used regularly by the mass media. Some examples of this are advertising slogans and newspaper headlines. Write the standfirst (the introductory paragraph) for these two newspaper articles.

Candle shop owner incensed!

Entranced by new doors!

Activity 3

Create other humorous headlines using **puns**, from other homographs, e.g. desert, object, produce, second.

| Lesson 6 | **Electronic revolution** |

Definitions/Key words

The '**electronic revolution**' has influenced the way in which we communicate. **New technologies,** such as mobile phones and the internet, have changed how the English language is used.

emoticons: the small faces commonly used to show emotions, e.g .;-) happy   :-/ uncertain

Activity 1

Look at the following text messages. What can you say about how messaging uses the conventions of the English language?

R u going out 18r?   *Informal style. Uses text abbreviations and words containing numbers.*

Want to c u again.
Wanna go out wid me?

Happy bday. Luv Sarah
;-)

Activity 2

Email messages are different from written letters in many ways. Look at the email overleaf and list the ways in which this differs from a conventional, written letter.

Activity 3

Complete the table overleaf with your observations of the language of text messages and emails in comparison to that of spoken and written language.

What do you notice about the distinctions between spoken and written language?

Email	
From:	"Louise Cameron" loucameron@e-world.com
To:	briggsjf@mail.com
Subject:	sat night
Date:	Wed, 23 Feb 2003 11:45:12

Jen
Gr8 to hear from u. What r u doing sat night? Some old pals
from uni are visiting. Having a few drinks round ours at about
7 ish. You up for it?
Lou
p.s. Macca will be there too - remember him?!

	New technologies	Written language	Spoken language
Formality			
Use of images, text and sound	rely on a combination of text, image and sound		
Lexical choices			
Spelling			
Grammatical constructions		generally follow the grammatical conventions of the English Language	
Punctuation			
Use of greeting and farewell			varies according to the relationship between the participants

Lesson 7   Accent & dialect

Definitions/Key words

accent: how words are pronounced
dialect: the form of a language spoken in one area which can involve different words, in sentences constructed differently and with different expressions

Activity 1

List as many different accents as you can. Look at these words and the way in which Geordies pronounce them. Have a go at saying them aloud.

burst	**borst**
brown	**broon**
church	**chorch**
four	**fower**
go	**gan**
house	**hoos**
know	**knaa**
with	**wiv**

In recent years, call centres and advertisements have tended to use people with distinctive accents. Why do you think this is the case?

Activity 2

Dialect is the regional variation that affects the way in which someone communicates. This can be evident through lexis and grammar. Examine the following examples of Geordie dialect. For each one, comment on the differences from Standard English in terms of lexis and grammar:

Howway an' see the gissies. *(Come and see the pigs.)*

Give ower howkin' yor sneck. *(Stop picking your nose.)*

Aa'll learn ye. *(I will teach you.)*

Activity 3

Many prose and poetry texts contain some form of dialect; from D. H. Lawrence novels which have some regional dialect from the Midlands to Irvine Welsh who writes entirely in the Glaswegian dialect. List the advantages and disadvantages of writing in dialect.

<table>
<tr><td></td><td></td></tr>
</table>

Lesson 8	**Pragmatics**

Definitions/Key words	**pragmatics**: the area of study which examines the factors that govern our choice of language in social interaction and the effects of our choice on others

Activity 1	List all the additional factors you can, which you think could influence the language choices in each of the following situations:

- A group of friends chatting in the sixth form centre.
- A parent reprimanding their child.
- A job interview.
- A telephone conversation with a sibling.

Activity 2	Pragmatics is also referred to as context-dependent meaning. It covers the following areas:

- The purpose or intention of the speaker or writer and the effect of their contribution on the listener or reader.
- The relationship between the participants.
- The participants' wider contextual knowledge and understanding of the world.
- The context of the topic and the constraints which apply in that situation.
- The personality of individual participants.
- The theories and concepts of conversation and genre (such as the cooperative principle and Grice's maxims).

Give examples of how and when any of these factors affect your own everyday interactions.

Activity 3	Have a look at the extracts on the following page. Can you find any examples of the factors listed above? Annotate the examples.

Headteacher:	Morning Jones. Come and sit down.
Jones:	Thank you, Sir.
Headteacher:	Right...do you know why you are here?
Jones:	Yes, Sir.
Headteacher:	Well, what do you have to say for yourself?

All you can eat for just £5.99
Monday – Friday
between 12pm and 2pm only

FAO: J. Bell

Can you please send a copy of the report
a.s.a.p. as I need to contact social
services today.

If you can foresee any problems with that,
call me and let me know.

Many thanks,

Darren Leonard

Can JK Rowling maintain Harry Potter's appeal? Nicholas Lezard takes a look at her long-awaited new volume.

Under her spell

So, is this a childish phenomenon or an adult one? One may be arrested, as I was, by the image, during a break in the TV coverage of a cricket match, of an MCC member about a third of the way through *The Order of the Phoenix* (this some 12 hours after the book's publication); but truly the extraordinary thing about it is that it is not all that extraordinary.

From *The Guardian Review*, 28.06.03

Lesson 1	**Phonology**

Definitions/Key words   **phonology**: the study of sound, concerning both the phonemes and prosodic features of the English language

Activity 1   Read the list of words shown in the table. Say each one aloud and then classify them into one of three categories according to their sound: positive, negative and neutral.

flashing	tumult	sacred
burst	measureless	seething
mazy	sinuous	ancestral
savage	chasm	dulcimer
wailing	chaffy	dread

Activity 2   Add two more words to each list. Discuss why the words sound harsh or soft, negative or neutral. Think about the effect of vowel sounds and harsh consonants in words.

Hint! Think about the phonemes which make words sound harsh, such as ck, t, g, and so on. You could also consider vowel sounds, particularly elongated vowel sounds such as oo or ee, which make words sound softer.

Activity 3   Read the poem *Kubla Khan* by Samuel Taylor Coleridge (next page). Discuss how the words sound and how this changes your perception of the poem and its meaning.

Kubla Khan
by Samuel Taylor Coleridge

In Xanadu did Kubla Khan
A stately pleasure-dome decree:
Where Alph, the sacred river, ran
Through caverns measureless to man
Down to a sunless sea.

So twice five miles of fertile ground
With walls and towers were girdled round:
And there were gardens bright with sinuous rills,
Where blossomed many an incense-bearing tree;
And here were forests ancient as the hills,
Enfolding sunny spots of greenery.
But oh! that deep romantic chasm which slanted
Down the green hill athwart a cedarn cover!
A savage place! as holy and enchanted
As e'er beneath a waning moon was haunted
By woman wailing for her demon-lover!
And from this chasm, with ceaseless turmoil seething,
As if this earth in fast thick pants were breathing,
A mighty fountain momently was forced:
Amid whose swift half-intermitted burst
Huge fragments vaulted like rebounding hail,
Or chaffy grain beneath the thresher's flail:
And 'mid these dancing rocks at once and ever
It flung up momently the sacred river.
Five miles meandering with a mazy motion
Through wood and dale the sacred river ran,
Then reached the caverns measureless to man,
And sank in tumult to a lifeless ocean:
And 'mid this tumult Kubla heard from far
Ancestral voices prophesying war!

The shadow of the dome of pleasure
Floated midway on the waves;
Where was heard the mingled measure
From the fountain and the caves.
It was a miracle of rare device,
A sunny pleasure-dome with caves of ice!
A damsel with a dulcimer
In a vision once I saw:
It was an Abyssinian maid,
And on her dulcimer she played,
Singing of Mount Abora
Could I revive within me
Her symphony and song
To such a deep delight 'twould win me,
That with music loud and long
I would build that dome in air,
That sunny dome! those caves of ice!
And all who heard should see them there,
And all should cry, Beware! Beware!
His flashing eyes, his floating hair!
Weave a circle round him thrice,
And close your eyes with holy dread,
For he on honey-dew hath fed.
And drunk the milk of Paradise.

Lesson 2   Phonemes

Definitions/Key words   **phonemes**: the smallest unit of sound in any given language

Activity 1   Look at the two groups of words shown below. Identify any similarities or connections between the words in each group. Find at least two more words to add to each group.

Hint! You are looking for connections concerning both (a) meaning and (b) sound.

Group 1	trudge	sludge	drudge	smudge

Group 2	snort	snigger	snide	sneer

Activity 2   Examine the selection of consonant clusters. Some combine to create one phoneme (which are they?). Choose one cluster and, using a dictionary to help you, find a group of words connected by your chosen sound. Remember to also look for words that are related in meaning, not just ones that contain the same cluster.

sn-	-ch	gr-	-sh	cr-	-ck

Activity 3   Look at this extract from *Much Ado about Nothing* by William Shakespeare. Remember that this has been written to be spoken. It contains many of the consonant sound patterns that you have just explored. Read the extract aloud, putting particular emphasis on the sounds where you think it is appropriate. What can you tell about Beatrice's feelings from the words which she chooses?

> Beatrice:
> Is he not approved in the height a villain, that hath slandered, scorned, dishonoured my kinswoman? O that I were a man! What, bear her in hand, until they come to take hands, and then with public accusation, uncover slander, unmitigated rancour? Oh God that I were a man! I would eat his heart in the market place.
> (Act 4, Scene 1, 291 – 295)

Lesson 3   Assonance

Definitions/Key words   **assonance:** recurring vowel sounds in words using different consonants (vowel rhyme)

Activity 1   Read the word cards below carefully. Classify them into one of two groups: long vowel sounds or short vowel sounds.
For example, **ate** has a long vowel sound and **cat** has a short vowel sound.

across	b**i**nd	br**i**dge	fl**e**ck
c**u**e	**a**te	sn**a**ke	s**ee**
gn**o**me	**i**ce	m**u**tter	d**o**g
dr**ea**m	**u**nder	sl**i**p	**o**range
uniq**ue**	**e**gg	br**o**ke	c**a**t

Activity 2   Check your understanding of the word assonance. Split into 2 groups: group 1 must write a sentence or phrase demonstrating assonance for each long vowel sound (a, e, i, o, u) and group 2 must write a sentence or a phrase demonstrating assonance for each short vowel sound.
For example:
> The c**a**t s**a**w the r**a**t **a**s the tr**a**p sn**a**pped shut.
> The sn**ai**l tr**ai**led l**a**zily over the p**a**le gr**ey** ground.

Activity 3   Discuss the effect of long and short vowel sounds. Think about the following ideas:

- what would be your definition of **assonance** following this exercise?
- when you say that language 'flows', what do you actually mean?

Lesson 4   Rhyme

Definitions/Key words   **rhyme**: created when the terminal phonemes in a word are identical to another word

Activity 1   Examine the list of words below. Complete the second column by writing down at least two words which rhyme with the word in column one.

fine	
wind	
rough	cuff, tough
bough	
sheer	
flow	
pear	
route	

Activity 2   Discuss why you think these particular words were chosen for Activity 1. Using your understanding of phonology explain what is meant when we say that a word *rhymes* with another.

What is meant, therefore, by 'half rhyme' or 'para rhyme'?

Activity 3   Select (from library or internet) an example of one of the text types listed below, and then find instances of rhyme, half-rhyme and no rhyme. Note at least two reasons why a writer might choose to use rhyme or half-rhyme in their composition.

- The lyrics of a verse of a popular song.
- An extract from one of Shakespeare's plays.
- A pre-1900 poem.
- A contemporary poem.

Lesson 5   Onomatopoeia

Definitions/Key words   **onomatopoeia:** when the sound of a word imitates the meaning.

Activity 1   Examine the sound bubbles below. The words are presented in the style of a comic strip. What is happening to the characters in the comic? How do you know?

Activity 2   Now, complete this table with five onomatopoeic words to describe each situation.

(1) The sound of children playing in a swimming pool	(2) Dropping a soluble aspirin into a glass of liquid	(3) The school canteen when the bell goes for lunch	(4) Walking in deep snow/leaves
	fizz		crunch

Activity 3   In this narrative, some words have been omitted. Fill in the gaps with your choice of onomatopoeic words and explain the meaning they add to the text.

I returned to a vacant house. I had to force the door as the stack of mail that had slowly gathered behind it_____ across the floor. The rancid stench of emptiness hung in the air. The eerie silence was only ruptured by the sharp _____ of the old grandfather clock that stood ominously in the dark hallway.

I turned to pick up the milk that had been souring on the doorstep. The bottles_____ together. It was then that I noticed the letter. My name was written neatly in black ink on the crisp white envelope. There was no stamp. Tentatively I opened it. The paper _____ in my hands as I started to tremble.

Lesson 6   Prosody

Definitions/Key words

prosody: the way in which something is said.
prosodic features: include **intonation**, **volume**, **pitch** and **pace**

Activity 1

Choose an emotion, for example: fear, anxiety, joy, jealousy… Now count from one to ten but use your voice to convey the emotion whilst you are counting. Don't tell anyone which emotion you are demonstrating, see if they can guess from your intonation!

Activity 2

Situation 1: A teacher talking to a pupil with whom he is angry.

Situation 2: A pet owner talking to their dog.

Situation 3: Someone chatting to his/her mate in the pub.

Situation 4: A mother talking to her small child.

Consider the four situations above. In each case, work out who has authority or is in control of the situation.

If you overheard a conversation between the teacher and the pupil, you would know that the teacher has the authority because the pupil addresses him as 'Sir'. Note down at least three other ways in which you might know who is in control from listening to a conversation between them (refer to the prosodic features above).

Activity 3

Often, the tone of voice that someone uses can alter the meaning of what they say. Look at the phrases shown in the speech bubbles. In what tone of voice do you think that the people in situations 1-4 might say these phrases? Have a go at saying them aloud and list some adverbs to describe their tone of voice.

Lesson 7   Pace and volume

Definitions/Key words   **pace, volume, pauses**

Activity 1   Choose one of the scenarios overleaf and read it aloud. Before you do, you will make choices about (a) how quickly and (b) how loudly each person speaks, based upon the meaning that you attach to that situation. Make some quick notes on what influenced your decisions for both (a) and (b). For example, *the robbers might be speaking quietly at first, but then become louder as they become more anxious.*

Activity 2   When studying spoken language, pauses are often just as revealing as the words that are said. Micro pauses are shown by this symbol (.) and longer pauses show the number of seconds within the brackets, (0.5), (4).

Look back at your scenario. Read it aloud again and decide where the speaker would pause and for how long. Text mark your script with these pauses.

Activity 3   Complete the table shown below. The columns are headed with **volume, pace** and **number of pauses**. At the top of each column you should write down possible situations where you would use maximum volume, pace or pauses. Work down each column, working towards situations where you would use less volume, pace and pauses.

	Volume	**Pace**	**No. of pauses**
+ **max**			If you were in a new situation for the first time where you were unsure about what you were doing, for example, the first day of your new job.
- **min**	If you didn't want someone else to hear, for example, if you were telling a secret.		

Lesson 7   Scenarios for Activity 1

Mum: Come on then, love. Open the envelope.
Daughter: I can't. What if they are all U grades?
Mum: Just open it!
Daughter *(opening envelope):* Oh my! I don't believe it! Straight As' Mum! A for
                Geography, A for Biology and A for Maths! Three A grades!
                Quick, pass the phone! I've got to tell Dad...

Speaker 1:   I'm really sorry to hear about your Grandma. When is the funeral?
Speaker 2:   It's on Monday afternoon at St. Peter's church.
Speaker 1:   Do you want me to come with you?
Speaker 2:   Yeah. I'd really appreciate that. Thanks.
Speaker 1:   No problem.

Robber no. 1: Just put the money in the bag.
Robber no. 2: Do as he says. Now. Come on. Hurry up.
Cashier: All of it... even the coins?
Robber no. 2: Shut up. No one asked you to talk.
Robber no. 1: That's all of it. Let's go... quick, before someone sees us.

Teacher: What are you doing?
Pupil: Playing football, Sir.
Teacher: I can see that, Jones. What have I told you about playing
                football near my classroom?
Pupil: Told us not to, Sir.
Teacher: What? I can't hear you, boy. Speak up. What have I told you
                about playing football near my classroom?
Pupil: TOLD US NOT TO, SIR!!!
Teacher: Don't raise your voice to me, young man. Right, after school
                detention.
Pupil: But, Sir!

Lesson 1   # Graphology

Definitions/Key words   **graphology:** the visual features of a text

Activity 1   The following features can appear in a variety of texts: newspapers, posters, theatre programmes... Sort them into categories of your choice and give each category a title.

logo	italics	rhyme	dialect	alliteration
clauses	ellipsis	illustrations	slogan	colour
bullets	homophones	emoticons	abbreviations	modifiers
conjunctions	headings	diagrams	colloquialisms	font
captions	tables	footnotes	running heads	borders

Activity 2   Share your ideas with the class. Have you got the same categories as anyone else? Which category is the most obvious? You have probably noted the features that are linked to the visual appearance of the text. You may have known these at GCSE level as **presentational devices**. List these and make sure that you known what each one means.

Activity 3   Find one of the following texts and text mark the graphological features.

- A recipe.
- A cinema/theatre programme.
- A magazine article.
- A poster.

Lesson 2   Genre

Definitions/Key words   **genre:** a particular type or style of literature, art, film or music

Activity 1   Look at the eight different genres below. Which of the statements below are true of which genre? They may fit more than one genre.

1. A diary	5. A broadsheet newspaper
2. An advertisement	6. A web page
3. A tabloid newspaper	7. A poem
4. Prose from a novel	8. A recipe

…has dates at the top
…has dense text in fairly long paragraphs
…has spaced-out text interspersed with pictures
…uses slogans
…includes symbols or abbreviations
…includes a variety of different lettering and styles of font
…uses captions
…uses a range of graphological features to catch the reader's eye
…contains large and prominent illustrations
…is presented in columns
…uses bullet points and subheadings to break up the text

Activity 2   One of the reasons a text might use a logo is so that it can be universally recognised and associated with an organisation. List the graphological features mentioned above and consider why a writer/ page designer might use them.

Activity 3   Genres are not always straightforward - within a genre there are often subgenres. Take one of the genres from activity 1 and devise another five statements about the presentation of that text.

Lesson 3   **Typography**

Definitions/Key words   **typography**: the planning and selection of fonts for printing

Activity 1   Look at the six different types of font below. Note two qualities of each one which make it distinctive.

1. **Different fonts**

2. Different fonts

3. *Different fonts*

4. Different fonts

5. Different fonts

6. **Different fonts**

Activity 2   Fill in the following table with your choice of font (1-6) and an explanation for your choice.

	Font	Explanation
A children's nursery		
A law firm		
A museum		
An I.T. company		
A fancy dress shop		
A garden centre		

Activity 3   Find an article from each of the following types of magazine and explain why they might have used the fonts they have.

- A magazine from a Sunday newspaper.
- A magazine aimed at teenage girls.
- A computer magazine.

Lesson 4	**Layout**
Definitions/Key words	**layout, design**

Activity 1   Look at the three texts shown on the following page. The layout of each is very different. Why? How does it affect the meaning of the text? Discuss with a partner.

Activity 2   (Working on a computer is recommended here.)
Often, poets who write specifically for children will play around with the presentation of their work as this makes their poetry more fun to read. Advertisers also experiment with layout in order to catch the audience's eye and to make their product stand out from others.

Either: choose one of the topics below and write a short verse, aimed at children. Present your poem on the page in an original way that reflects the meaning.

> • Trees in Autumn
> • Pick 'n' mix sweets
> • Space
> • A desert island

or: write some advertising copy for an imaginary new confectionary product. Again, reflect meaning in presentation.

Activity 3   Write a short commentary which accompanies your poem or advertisement. Explain what effect you intended to have on your reader and address your choice of lexis, grammar, syntax and graphology.

Text 1: **Little Fish** by D H Lawrence

Little Fish

The tiny fish enjoy themselves
in the sea
Quick splinters of life,
their little lives are fun to them
in the sea

Text 2: from the *Oxford Concise Medical Dictionary*

bruise (contusion) n. an area of skin discoloration caused by the escape of blood from ruptured underlying vessels following injury. Initially red or pink, a bruise gradually becomes bluish, and then greenish yellow, as the haemoglobin in the tissues breaks down chemically and is absorbed. It may be necessary to draw off blood from very severe bruises through a needle to aid healing.

bruit *n.* see MURMUR

Text 3: **A Taste of Honey** by Shelagh Delaney

SCENE TWO

JO *and her* BOY FRIEND, *a coloured naval rating, walking on the street. They stop by the door.*

JO: I'd better go in now. Thanks for carrying my books.
BOY: Were you surprised to see me waiting outside school?
JO: Not really.
BOY: Glad I came?
JO: You know I am.
BOY: So am I.
JO: Well, I'd better go in.
BOY: Not yet! Stay a bit longer.
JO: All right! Doesn't it go dark early? I like winter. I like it better than all the other seasons.
BOY: I like it too. When it goes dark early it gives me more time for -
    [*He kisses her.*]

Lesson 5	Juxtaposition

Definitions/Key words

juxtaposition: when images and/or texts are placed side by side

Activity 1

Examine the following statements which headline articles about the plight of the children of drug addicts. Using your knowledge of syntax and lexis, summarise the connotations of two or more statements.

Innocent victims suffer this tragic addiction
The druggie generation
The heroin legacy
Families affected by evil social disease
Children of drugs
Support these desperate families
'Irresponsible' mothers

Activity 2

Imagine that there are two pictures to accompany these articles:

A female who is gaunt and pale with dark eyes. She is holding a small child who is wrapped in a grubby blanket.

The same small child, dressed cleanly in a red coat, grasping a teddy bear.

Which of the above images would you juxtapose with each headline? Why?

Activity 3

Imagine that you have been asked to design a leaflet warning young people against the dangers of drug abuse. Mark on a piece of A4 paper where you would place each of the following and explain your decision:

• Help line phone number
• Statistics on drug related deaths
• The first image mentioned above
• An emotive slogan/ title
• The second image mentioned above
• A case history of a recovered drug addict